CHRISTIE'S
COLLECTABLES

CHRISTIE'S
COLLECTABLES

SMALL SILVER TABLEWARE

Stephen Helliwell

LITTLE, BROWN AND COMPANY
BOSTON NEW YORK LONDON TORONTO

A LITTLE, BROWN BOOK

FIRST PUBLISHED IN GREAT BRITAIN IN 1996
BY LITTLE, BROWN AND COMPANY (UK)

CONCEIVED, EDITED AND DESIGNED BY
MARSHALL EDITIONS
170 PICCADILLY LONDON W1V 9DD

A CIP catalogue record for this book is available
from the British Library.

ISBN 0-316-87785-9

2 4 6 8 10 9 7 5 3 1

EDITOR GWEN RIGBY
DESIGNERS FRANCES DE REES, HELEN SPENCER
PICTURE EDITOR ELIZABETH LOVING

Marshall Editions would like to thank
Edward Schneider of Christie's Images for his help
in the creation of this book.

Origination by HBM Print Pte, Singapore
Printed and bound in Portugal by Printer Portuguesa

LITTLE, BROWN AND COMPANY (UK)
Brettenham House Lancaster Place London WC2E 7EN

CHRISTIE'S
8 King Street St. James's London SW1Y 6QT

CHRISTIE'S SOUTH KENSINGTON
85 Old Brompton Road London SW7 3LD

CHRISTIE'S
502 Park Avenue New York NY 10022

CHRISTIE'S AUSTRALIA
298 New South Head Road Double Bay Sydney NSW 2028

CHRISTIE'S SOUTH AFRICA
P.O. Box 72126 Parkview Johannesburg 2122

CHRISTIE'S JAPAN
Sankyo Ginza Building 6-5-13 Ginza Chuo-ku Tokyo 104

Contents

PRICE CODES

The following price codes are used in this book:
£A Less than £100 **£B** £101–£500
£C £501–£1,000 **£D** £1,001–£2,000 **£E** £2,001–£5,000
£F £5,001–£10,000 **£G** More than £10,000

Unless otherwise stated, the first price given refers to the value
of an individual example of any of the items illustrated.

Valuation is an imprecise art and prices can vary for many
reasons, including the condition of a piece, fashion and national and
regional interest. Prices given in this book are approximate
and based on likely *auction* values. *Insurance* values reflect the
retail replacement price and as such are liable to be higher.

Introduction

*S*ILVER IS ONE OF THE MOST VERSATILE OF NATURAL materials, and its extreme malleability has enabled silversmiths to create a wide range of wares, both beautiful and functional, for use on the table.

*I*nitially silver was primarily appreciated for its bullion value. Goods were often pawned or melted down, and many splendid pieces were "recycled", with old-fashioned wares part-exchanged for modern pieces. As late as the 19th century, few admired the simplicity of antique silver, and the elegant lines of many fine pieces were later lost beneath chased flowers and foliage.

Collecting silver is a relatively new phenomenon, and there is now a steady market for fine tableware. The price of good pieces has kept up with inflation, and silver has been a less risky investment than many other types of antiques; yet even a collector of limited means can still find fine items by scouring auction rooms and antique shops.

Pure silver is too soft to stand up to use, so it is alloyed with other metals, mainly copper, to increase its durability. British silver is generally of "sterling standard", the alloy made up from 92.5 percent pure silver and 7.5 percent base metal. In the late 17th century the edges of silver coins were clipped, the tiny pieces melted down and then sold as bullion. To counteract this

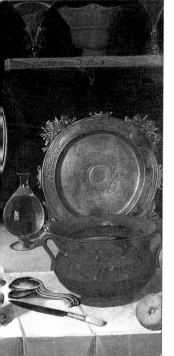

The Spanish artist Juan Bautista de Espinosa painted this still life in 1624, probably as a record of some grandee's fine and precious collection of tableware. This included silver-gilt salvers, a silver fluted cup, salt cellars, knives, spoons and forks in the style of the period.

The dining table at the English country house Charlecote Park is set with fine Georgian silver.

malpractice, in 1697 a new "Britannia standard" was introduced, containing 95.8 percent pure silver. But Britannia silver was too soft to withstand even normal wear, and in 1720 Britain reverted to sterling. Most American silver is also of sterling standard, but the silver content of pieces in some European countries can be as low as 80 percent.

Although silver had to be alloyed, there was always the temptation to defraud the buyer. And as early as 1300 buyers of silver in Britain were given some protection, when the first hallmark, a crowned leopard's head, was stamped on goods to indicate that they had been assayed and found to be of sterling standard. In 1363, makers were obliged to stamp their products with personal marks, enabling faulty goods to be traced back to their source. At first, these marks took the form of symbols. By the late 1500s the first two letters of the surname were used; these were replaced in the 1720s by the initial letters of both first name and surname.

*I*n 1463 the date letter was added, the letters changing each year in cycles of about 20 years. A fourth mark, the lion passant, was introduced in 1544, and the crowned leopard became the mark for London to show royal control of the assay office. Other British offices used various symbols, such as a castle and a thistle for Edinburgh and a harp for Dublin. During the Britannia standard period of 1697 to 1720, the lion passant was replaced by the figure of Britannia, and the leopard's head by a lion's head in profile; these marks disappeared

Less expensive than silver, electroplated wares were produced in quantity specifically for middle-class buyers.

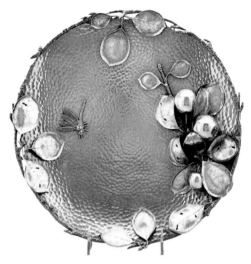

Silver has been combined with bronze and gilding on this beautiful early Art Nouveau piece.

with the reintroduction of sterling standard. In 1784 silver was taxed at sixpence per ounce, and a new mark – the head of the monarch in profile – was introduced to show that the tax had been paid. This mark disappeared when the duty was removed in 1890.

*I*n Europe, each country employed its own system of hallmarking, while in America some early pieces carried facsimiles of British marks, although later wares often bear the word "coin", denoting that they were made from silver of the standard set by the U.S. mint, established in 1776. In 1868 America adopted the British standard and wares were stamped "sterling"; many bore the full maker's name, and some later pieces had patent dates also. Old Sheffield plate, first produced in 1743, was occasionally marked, but electroplated wares, first made commercially by George and Frederick Elkington in the mid-1800s, often bear no stamps.

TIPS FOR COLLECTORS

• Despite all the precautions of hallmarking, many fakes were, and still are, produced – some clumsily obvious, others difficult to spot.

• Although it is illegal to reproduce hallmarks, "soft punches", or homemade stamps, are sometimes used, and marks may be removed from genuine antiques and let into fakes. Inspect pieces carefully to ensure that there are no soldered joints hidden by plating.

• Conversions, such as adding a spout to a mug to form a jug, contravene the laws of hallmarking. Check any added silver; it should be assayed and separately marked if up to standard.

• Examine the fluted bowls of ladles or butter dishes carefully; splits along the chased lines have often been mended and the repair covered up with plating.

• Where ladles with plain bowls have been converted to shell bowls, the fluted lines look "sharp", lacking the wear caused by use and cleaning.

• Initials on later pieces of silver are unwelcome, but those on early wares add to the value.

• Pairs or sets are usually more valuable than single items, and an original case enhances a piece's value.

An early example of fine workmanship, this silver-gilt wine cup, the bowl chased with a stylized floral design, was made in London in 1612.

Apostle spoon

THE PRACTICE OF SETTING A TABLE with flatware, or cutlery, dates only from the late 17th century. Before that, knives and spoons were personal possessions, the latter often given as christening or betrothal presents. Spoons dating from the 15th century are often badly or incompletely hallmarked, although many are crudely engraved with the initials of the original recipient and the date of presentation.

THE EARLIEST SPOONS THAT HAVE survived were constructed with cast and chased terminals soldered on to the slender stems. These terminals were modelled as Apostles, baluster vases, lions and various figures. While Apostle spoons were undoubtedly sold individually, they were also made in sets of 12, representing the Apostles, with a larger "Master" spoon depicting Christ. It is almost impossible to find a set still together, and even good single examples have become extremely expensive.

THIS SPOON, MADE IN LONDON IN 1490 AND BEARING an unknown maker's mark – a Gothic "L" – would appear to be part of the earliest recorded hallmarked set of Apostle spoons. Its gilt terminal depicts St. James the Greater.

Length 7¼in/18.5cm   £G

12

Slip-top spoons

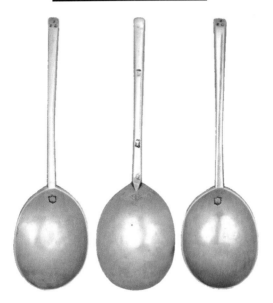

*JEREMY JOHNSON OF LONDON MADE THESE
simple slip-top spoons in 1652. The slender stem
has no terminal but ends in an angled plane.
Although slip-top spoons are sometimes known as
"Puritan spoons", there is little evidence that
the terminals of Apostle spoons were removed
to create them. It is likely that they were
simply a less expensive alternative to those with
cast terminals. Such spoons are marked
with a single stamp in the bowl and the other
marks on the narrow stem.*

*FAKES OF ALL EARLY SPOONS HAVE BEEN MADE, SOMETIMES
by casting from originals, more often by adding
new cast terminals to later spoons. The latter are
easy to spot by examining the hallmarks.*

Length 6¼in/16cm   £C; set of 6 £G

Trefid spoon

In the mid-17th century the style of flatware changed enormously under the influence of fashions from France. Spoons were made from one piece of hammered sheet silver, with the most vulnerable point where the bowl met the stem reinforced with an additional small mount soldered into place. This soon became known as the "rat-tail" because of its shape.

As production on a larger scale became possible, sets of spoons of different sizes were made. The earliest examples had plain slightly flaring handles with simple cut-off ends. By the 1680s, the ends of the handles were shaped into more elaborate forms, the most typical being the Trefid depicted here.

Although many examples were left plain, others were decorated with stamped or engraved scrolling foliage on both the front of the handle and the reverse of the bowl. Many also have engraved initials and dates, although by this time the hallmarks are much easier to read, since the stamps were all punched on the broader stem.

This Trefid spoon was made at Plymouth, England, by one of the many prolific West Country silversmiths, John Murch. Although it has no date letter it bears an inscription dated 1700.

Length 6½in/16.5cm £C

Dognose flatware

FASHIONS CHANGED AGAIN AS THE 17TH CENTURY
progressed. The central lobe of the Trefid pattern
grew, while the smaller lobes disappeared, resulting in
the simpler "dognose" pattern. By the early 1700s,
forks – available since c.1632, but only in limited
use – had become accepted. Full table services were
produced, often on a huge scale. Knives were made
with a "cannon" or, more commonly, "pistol" silver
handle inset with a scimitar-shaped iron blade.

THE FORKS SHOWN HERE WERE MADE IN 1701 BY
Isaac Davenport, London, the spoons in 1702 by
David Willaume I, a silversmith of Huguenot descent,
also of London. The knives bear an indistinct
maker's mark and date from the early 1700s.

Length spoons 7½in/19cm

£A; sets of 6 £E (spoons and forks), £D (knives)

Hanoverian pattern

The Hanoverian pattern evolved from the dognose pattern, the end of the handle being rounded off to make an even simpler form. It proved tremendously popular, remaining in vogue until c.1770. Revived in the late 19th century, this elegant style is still produced.

Hanoverian pattern spoons made before c.1730 have rat-tail strengtheners, while later specimens have smaller rounded heels or drops. Some were also stamped with Rococo scrolling, foliage, flowers and shells. So-called fancy-back teaspoons were decorated with political motifs or designs celebrating peace and prosperity or Britain's naval supremacy. Good examples with sharp details are much sought after today.

Until the third quarter of the 18th century, tables were laid with the reverse of spoon and fork handles uppermost to display the crests and armorials of their owners. This tablespoon and fork are part of a set in the Hanoverian pattern made by John Jacob, London, in 1735 and 1736 and engraved with the arms of George, second Earl of Warrington.

Length spoon 7¾in/20cm   £A; set of 12 pairs £G

Old English pattern

FIRST SEEN IN THE 1760s, this pattern overlapped the Hanoverian pattern by some 20 years. The two differ only slightly – the Old English spoon handles turn down instead of up, the result of a change in fashion which dictated that spoon bowls and fork tines should face upward on the table. Since engravers needed a flat surface for their customers' armorials, the spoon handles were reversed.

IN 1784, WHEN AN EXTRA HALLMARK appeared to show that a new duty on silver had been paid, the hallmarks were moved to the broader part of the handles. By the 1780s most forks had acquired a fourth tine.

WHILE PIECES IN THE OLD ENGLISH PATTERN were usually left plain, some had stamped beaded or reeded borders or bright-cut engraving, and the silver-gilt items here, made by the cutlery specialists George Smith and William Fearn of London, in 1793, have engraved feather-edge borders.

THE KNIFE WAS MADE BY MOSES BRENT of London, who specialized in knife handles. Two stamped halves were soldered together and filled with pitch for strength and weight.

Length dessert spoon 7in/18cm

£A; sets of 6 £B

Fiddle pattern

THE NAME OF THIS PATTERN DERIVES FROM THE violin-shaped handles. It was popular in France from c.1750, and remained in favour for many decades. Although the pattern appeared in Britain in the mid-18th century, early examples are rare, and it was first produced in large quantities c.1800.

THIS STURDY AND IMPRESSIVE STYLE SOON OUSTED THE lighter, more elegant Old English pattern from popularity, but today plain Fiddle pattern has become the cheapest antique flatware on the market, especially if it is engraved with initials.

ALTHOUGH A COMPOSITE SET WILL NEVER BE AS valuable as a "straight" set all by the same maker, it is possible over a period of time to assemble a canteen made by different makers at a cost which is little more than the current bullion value of the silver.

THE LARGE GERMAN SPOON (TOP), WITH A slightly waisted grip, bears the maker's name: "Cahn", c.1880; the British tablespoon (above) was made by J. Muir Jnr., Glasgow, in 1841; and the small nielloed spoon (left) was produced in Moscow in 1887.

Length British spoon 8¾in/22cm £A

Fiddle pattern variations

WHILE PLAIN FIDDLE PATTERN CUTLERY REMAINS unpopular, decorated Fiddle pattern is in great demand. It is mainly sought by collectors trying to build up a table service as inexpensively as possible – and certainly at a lower price than a modern table service.

If a collector has the patience to assemble a composite canteen by the same maker, it will prove much more valuable than a mixed set, even if the dates differ.

THREE VARIATIONS OF THE BASIC PATTERN appear here: a William IV Fiddle and Thread salt spoon by William Eley, London, 1836; a Victorian Fiddle, Thread and Shell teaspoon by George Adams, London, 1842; and an American electroplated Fiddle and Shell dessert fork with untraced marks, c.1870.

Length fork 8¼in/21cm £A

The mark of
George Adams, *c.*1858

King's & Queen's patterns

Two more important flatware designs appeared in the early 1800s – King's and Queen's patterns. Both have rounded and waisted handles and are decorated with shells and scrolling foliage, but King's pattern is slightly less ornate and heavy, with a simple double leaf stamped on the handle. Queen's pattern has a large flower head with foliage in the same position. Many variations of both patterns were produced during the 1800s.

Both designs can be double-struck, with the pattern on both sides, or single-struck (using thinner silver), with the pattern only on the upper surface. Single-struck flatware was usually made in Edinburgh or Glasgow and sells for about two-thirds the price of double-struck.

The table forks are both Queen's pattern. The top one was made in 1852 by W. Crouch and Sons, Glasgow, the other by Ball, Black and Co., New York, 1851–76. The King's pattern dessert spoon is by Robert Wallis, London, 1843.

Length forks 8in/20cm
£A; set of 6 £B

Double Shell & Laurel

Many more elaborate flatware designs were produced in the first half of the 19th century, using handle outlines of the King's shape. These include King's Honeysuckle, Dolphin, Princess and the splendid Double Shell and Laurel. Made from a complex die, it includes both convex and concave shells, honeysuckle and laurel leaves, and was produced only in the workshop of the celebrated London silversmith Paul Storr, who worked from 1792 until 1838.

Storr's career covered both the Regency and George IV periods, when fashion dictated the use of sumptuous silver, often enriched with gilding. Although this was employed partly for its decorative effect, it was also practical, the thin gold "wash" protecting the silver from the harmful effects of fruit acids. Silver-gilt was, therefore, used more for dessert pieces such as these spoons, made in 1813.

The mark of
Paul Storr, 1795

P.S

Length 7¼in/18.5cm
£A; set of 6 £B

Stag Hunt pattern

*THE KING'S SHAPE WITH ITS MANY VARIATIONS WAS
popular during the 19th century, and many
versions are still produced, including the Stag Hunt
pattern (above). The rarer Fox Hunt and Boar
Hunt patterns are no longer regularly made. These
patterns feature hounds and huntsmen and their
prey, as well as finely detailed masks struck on the
backs of the spoon bowls. They were designed
by Thomas Stothard for the London firm
of Rundell, Bridge and Rundell, a partnership that
included Paul Storr from 1807 to 1819.
ALTHOUGH ALL WERE INITIALLY PRODUCED ONLY BY STORR,
later examples by other London silversmiths
occasionally appear. The silver-gilt spoon and fork
here were made by Paul Storr in 1822, the plain
silver ones by William Eaton, London, in 1825.*

Length spoons 7¼in/18.5cm   £A; set of 6 £C

Pierced Vine pattern

IN THE 19TH CENTURY, SEVERAL KING'S SHAPE
patterns featuring vines were made. Dripping with
luscious fruit, all were used primarily for dessert
services, although some tablespoons and forks in the
Chased Vine and Pierced Vine patterns can be found,
and both patterns are still in production.

THE SILVER IN THIS ELABORATE PART DESSERT SERVICE IS
protected by a gilt wash. The pieces have handles
pierced with trailing vines and enhanced with cast
monograms and Russian Imperial eagles and crowns,
so the set must have been a private commission.

THE SPOONS AND FORKS BEAR HALLMARKS FOR MOSCOW IN
1847 and 1848, but the knives were produced
in London in 1845, which suggests that
they were taken to Russia, where local craftsmen
made faithful copies of the design.

Length spoon 8¼in/21cm £A; set of 6 £B

Tiffany dessert services 1

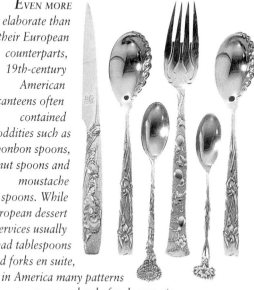

EVEN MORE elaborate than their European counterparts, 19th-century American canteens often contained oddities such as bonbon spoons, nut spoons and moustache spoons. While European dessert services usually had tablespoons and forks en suite, in America many patterns were used only for dessert pieces.

MANY OBJECTS WERE ALSO ENHANCED WITH parcel-gilt or frosted finishes, and silver and silver-gilt were even combined with metals such as copper and bronze, creating unusual objects in the Aesthetic taste, which was at its apogee in the 1870s.

A MIXTURE OF DIVERSE BUT LINKED DESIGNS IS TYPICAL of the Aesthetic period, when spontaneity was valued more highly than uniformity. The part dessert service (above), made in New York c.1880, is typical, with assorted flower terminals on the coffee spoons; ice cream spoons in the Iris pattern; pastry forks in the Vine pattern; and knives in the Pansy pattern.

Length knife 6¾in/17cm £A; set £E

Tiffany dessert services II

Following the visit of Commodore Perry to Japan in 1854, Oriental designs became hugely popular. Insects, birds in flight, fans, bamboo and prunus now smothered both cutlery and other silver pieces. In the part dessert service above, also c.1880, there are matted and frosted sections, Oriental motifs are applied in gilt to the handles, and geometric shapes decorate the blades, bowls and tines.

Length knife 8½in/21.5cm £A; set £E

The mark of
Tiffany & Co.
1854–70

Bacchanalian pattern

In the 19th century, the Bacchanalian pattern designed by Thomas Stothard for Rundell, Bridge and Rundell was used only for dessert services; today it is reproduced in all sizes of flatware. Original pieces were almost always gilt, although the thin gold skin may have disappeared after many years of cleaning.

Silver can be regilt by electroplating and a skilful silversmith can adjust the tone of the gilding by adding trace elements so that regilt pieces match the original colour. This part dessert set was made by John and Henry Lias, London, in 1873.

Length spoon 7¼in/18.5cm £A; set of 6 £B

Rich Figure pattern

FRANCIS HIGGINS AND SON OF LONDON WAS ONE *of the most prolific specialist cutlery makers of the 19th century, producing flatware of the highest quality. Francis Higgins, Jnr., is said to have walked around his factory with a hammer, to destroy any work that was not up to his exacting standards.*

WHEN HIGGINS FIRST INTRODUCED THE RICH FIGURE PATTERN, *pieces were made for it by Hunt and Roskell. This was common practice throughout the history of silversmithing, most makers specializing rather than producing a complete range of goods.*

THE PIECES ABOVE ARE PART OF A SILVER-GILT SERVICE *made in 1903 by Higgins and sold unmarked to its rivals Goldsmiths and Silversmiths Co. Ltd., who then added its own mark.*

Length spoon 7½in/19cm £A; set of 6 £B

Mistletoe dessert set

WHILE AMERICAN SILVERSMITHS PRODUCED MANY
*delightful novelties in silver, British craftsmen
preferred in the main to stick to easily saleable lines.
But labour was still relatively cheap, and
electroplating allowed the production of base-metal
novelty items in nickel, Britannia metal or German
silver covered with a thin skin of silver.*

THIS PARCEL-GILT ELECTROPLATED DESSERT SET, WITH
*four fruit-serving spoons and a sugar-sifting spoon,
was made by Mappin and Webb of Sheffield
c.1880 and may have been a Christmas gift,
since the handle terminals are cast in the form of
mistletoe leaves and berries. The set is still in
its plush and satin-lined tooled leather case; a case
in good condition can double the price of a set.*

Length serving spoons 9½in/24cm Set £B

American teaspoons

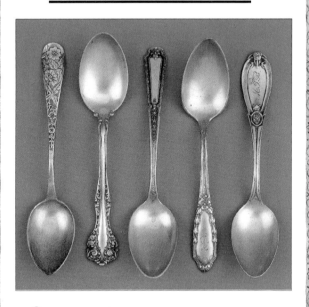

ONLY A FEW YEARS AGO, THESE SILVER TEASPOONS were bought in New York for $5 each. They illustrate the multitude of flatware designs produced by a host of American makers, most of whom failed to mark their wares.

THE FLORAL-DECORATED SPOON (FAR LEFT) WAS MADE c.1890 by Duhme and Co., Cincinnati, Ohio. The others are all impressed "sterling", and three have design patent dates of (left to right) 1924, 1910 and 1862. The initials on the undated spoon (far right) are engraved at a right angle to the handle; this is common in American silver flatware, but is not seen in Britain. Souvenir teaspoons are avidly collected in America, but in Europe odd teaspoons can still be bought for a few pounds each.

Length floral spoon 6in/15cm £A

Chased Vine pattern

Some Victorian dessert services were both elaborate in design and comprehensive, with a wide range of serving implements. Above is the top tray from a brass-bound coromandel-wood canteen, which also contains a dozen place settings with knives, forks and spoons. Each piece is engraved with two crests, indicating that the set was given as a wedding present. It is in mint condition, and can hardly have been used.

The entire set was made in silver-gilt in the Chased Vine pattern by Martin Hall and Co., Sheffield, in 1874, 1875 and 1879. The servers comprise a pair of fruit spoons, a sugar-sifting spoon, a cream ladle, a pair of grape scissors inset with steel blades and a cake slice and fork. The original plush-lined box adds enormously to the value of the set.

Length fruit spoon 7½in/19cm   Set £C

Edwardian dessert set

An inscription on the mahogany-veneered
canteen records that this splendid electroplated
Edwardian set was given to a factory manager on his
retirement in 1903. The set was made by Walker &
Hall of Sheffield, and the blades and prongs are
engraved and the silver ferrules hallmarked. It is in
unused condition, and the colours of the plush
and quilted satin linings are totally unfaded.
  Mother-of-pearl was commonly used for the
handles of both dessert knives and forks and fish
knives and forks at this time, and the collector
should examine them carefully, since the handles
often become loose through washing in hot water.

Length grape scissors 7¼in/18.5cm   Set £B

The mark of
Walker & Hall
1903

Dessert set & berry spoon

THE VICTORIANS OFTEN VIEWED PLAIN GEORGIAN *silver almost as a raw material, ruining many fine pieces by covering them with chased and embossed decoration. Such objects are usually worth far less today than their plain, original counterparts. The exception is so-called berry spoons, usually sold in pairs. These were commonly made from Fiddle or Old English pattern tablespoons, the bowls and handles of which were die-stamped and chased in relief with fruits. Matching sugar-sifting spoons, made from sauce ladles, can also be found.*

THE QUALITY OF THE FLIMSY BERRY SPOON (BELOW), MADE BY *Eley and Fearn, London, in 1800, should be compared with that of the heavy-gauge silver Bacchanalian pattern dessert set (above) made by John and Henry Lias, London, in 1880.*

Length sifting spoon 6¼in/16cm Set £B

Length berry spoon
8¼in/21cm £A

American dessert servers

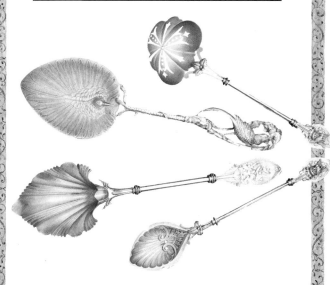

AS CAN BE SEEN FROM THESE PIECES, PART OF A
*larger set of nine, American dessert servers are
much more elaborate than their European
counterparts. The spoons are simply stamped
"sterling", with no maker's mark, but their design
suggests manufacture by the Whiting Manufacturing
Company in North Attleboro, Massachusetts,
or Newark, New Jersey, c.1870.*

ALL THE PIECES DIFFER, WITH VARYING TERMINALS OR
*bowl shapes. This diversity is typical of American
wares made in the second half of the 19th
century, but is rare in British flatware. The bird and
nest motif on some of the handle terminals is
echoed in the largest spoon, whose bowl is chased
with a stylized dove with outstretched wings,
its terminal modelled as a pheasant.*

Length 8–10¼in/20–26cm £A; set £D

British fish servers

SPECIAL SERVERS FOR FISH WERE SOON FOUND
to be necessary, since the strong flavour
often lingers, tainting other foodstuffs. But knives
and forks for eating fish did not appear until
the second half of the 19th century.

THE EARLIEST FISH SLICES WERE GENERALLY MADE IN
standard flatware patterns or with hollow,
knife-type handles filled with pitch, their blades
decorated with pierced and engraved designs,
often incorporating dolphins, boats and
other marine features. By the mid-1800s, ivory or
mother-of-pearl handles had become more common
and fish slices were often sold in a case
together with fish-serving forks. Engraving
also became increasingly elaborate.

THE PISTOL HANDLES ON THIS PAIR, MADE BY MARTIN HALL
and Co., Sheffield, in 1876, hark back to the
mid-18th century, when the style was first popular.
Length slice 9½in/24cm   Pair £B

American fish servers

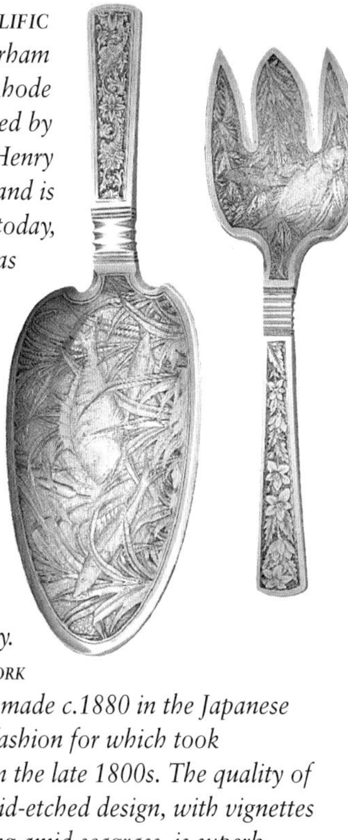

THE PROLIFIC company of Gorham of Providence, Rhode Island, was started by Jabez Gorham and Henry Webster in 1831 and is still manufacturing today, although it was bought by Textron Inc. in 1967.

THROUGHOUT ITS history, the firm was noted for the superior design and quality of its wares. Indeed, its finest pieces are equal to anything by its rival Tiffany.

THE FISH SLICE AND FORK shown here were made c.1880 in the Japanese taste, the fashion for which took America by storm in the late 1800s. The quality of the engraved and acid-etched design, with vignettes of fish swimming amid seagrass, is superb. Beautifully drawn and brilliantly executed, this ranks among the best of 19th-century work.

Length slice 10¾in/27cm   Pair £F

J. Gorham & Son

Gorham's mark c.1842; in 1863 the name changed to the Gorham Manufacturing Company.

Salad servers 1

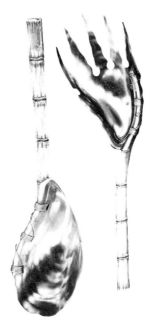

*N*ATURALISM WAS POPULAR THROUGHOUT THE
*second half of the 19th century, and the average
middle-class parlour contained wallpaper and
soft furnishings covered with larger than life flowers
and mahogany furniture carved with foliage.
Silver, too, was affected by this exuberance,
and silversmiths strove to make faithful copies of
flowers, animals, birds and seashells.*
*T*HIS SPLENDID PAIR OF SALAD SERVERS, ONE DATED FOR
*1890, the other for 1891, was made by
Gorham, Providence, Rhode Island. They are
modelled as shells lashed to bamboo stems,
with each detail hand-chased.*
Length spoon 9½in/24cm   Pair £D

Salad servers II

*ALTHOUGH PLAIN SILVER IS ATTRACTIVE IN ITS OWN
right, it can look particularly striking when
combined with enamel, base metal, ivory or wood.
THIS PAIR OF SALAD SERVERS MADE C.1920 BY THE WHITING
Manufacturing Company of Newark, New Jersey, is
a late example of the Aesthetic taste. The walnut
handles are finely carved, with chased silver
dragonflies applied, while the gilt-lined bowl and
tines are hammered and chased to resemble seashells.
IT IS UNUSUAL TO FIND JAPANESE-INFLUENCED PIECES STILL
being manufactured in the 1920s, but these may have
been made to match a customer's existing flatware
service or to replace lost or damaged items.*

Length spoon 10½in/26.5cm   Pair £D

Pickle forks

First introduced in the mid-19th century, pickle spoons and forks were initially produced in the more common flatware patterns. They closely resemble contemporary sugar spoons in size, and the bowls are cut into three or four broad tines.

Although useful for serving pickles from shallow dishes, they were too short to reach into the large cut-glass pickle jars popular from c.1860, and a new form of server evolved. Most had long ivory or mother-of-pearl handles, but all-silver examples are not uncommon.

By the late 1800s, forks with the outer tines shaped into tiny barbs had largely replaced spoons, although in the early 1900s some spoons had a central hole to allow liquid to drain away.

The rare combination olive spoon and fork, modelled as a coral branch, was made by Gorham, Providence, Rhode Island, c.1890; the ivory-handled pickle forks by Edward Hutton, London, in 1886.

Length pickle fork 8¾in/22cm
Pair £A; olive spoon £B

Bread fork & marrow scoop

In polite society in the 19th century, diners used large forks to help themselves to slices or rolls of bread. Bread forks, with their short handles, usually of ivory, and their flat, broad prongs, should not be confused with toasting forks, which have much longer, sometimes folding or telescopic handles.

This bread fork, made in 1890 by an unknown firm, R & S of Glasgow, was inspired by the work of the brilliant avant-garde designer Christopher Dresser. The stark lines foreshadowed Art Deco designs.

Length fork 6in/15cm £A

Roasted marrow bones were a popular savoury dish, and in the early 1700s long implements were devised to facilitate removal of the jelly. Most of these had two elongated bowls of different sizes, which usually faced the same way. Such marrow scoops are quite common; marrow spoons, with a scoop at one end and a tablespoon-sized bowl at the other, are rarer. This scoop was made in 1862 by the London flatware specialist Francis Higgins. £A

The mark of
Francis Higgins and Son,
London, 1903

Butter spades & knives

*U*SED FOR LESS THAN 50 YEARS FROM *the mid- to late 18th century, butter spades are rare. They have short, flat-pointed blades, which are often engraved with a crest and are always hallmarked on the back. Most had fruit-wood or ivory handles, which were often stained green in the 1780s and '90s. This one was made by George Smith and William Fearn, London, in 1795.*

Length 7in/18cm £B

*B*UTTER KNIVES SOON REPLACED SPADES. THEY, *too, usually had green-stained ivory handles, but from the early 1800s were made to match other flatware. Most were almost tablespoon size, but by the 1850s they had become smaller, with engraved scimitar-shaped blades fitted into ivory, agate, mother-of-pearl or die-stamped hollow silver handles. The knife below left was made by Thomas Shaw, Birmingham, 1833* (£A), *the one below right by John Daly, Dublin, 1795* (£A).

Serving tongs

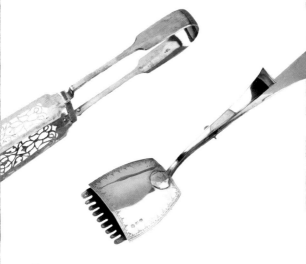

LARGE SERVING TONGS WERE FIRST MADE TOWARD
the end of the 1700s. For many years they were all
known as asparagus tongs, but it is now thought
that the narrow-bladed examples were used to serve
meat, since asparagus stalks would break when
lifted unless the blades were broader.

SOME EARLY TONGS OPERATED LIKE SCISSORS, WHILE OTHERS
were hinged at the end, rather like fire tongs. By the
1830s, however, most were made in an elongated
U shape, the curved end formed from silver that was
heated and beaten to give sufficient spring.

THE FIDDLE PATTERN TONGS (LEFT) ARE BY GEORGE ADAMS,
London, 1869. The much rarer pair (right),
by Carden Terry and Jane Williams, Dublin, 1807,
is sprung in the centre and engraved with
bright-cut stylized foliage; the tined lower blade
is a particularly unusual feature.

Length Irish tongs 11in/28cm £B (each piece)

Sugar nips & grape scissors

THE FIRST SUGAR TONGS, WITH plain straight shafts terminating in small bowls with rat-tails, were introduced in the late 1600s. They did not grip well, and by the 1720s scissor-action sugar nips had appeared, their pivots often crudely engraved with initials or crests. Bowls on the earliest examples retained the rat-tail, but by the 1740s most were a more practical Rococo shell shape. Sugar nips are difficult to date since few are fully marked; the pair above was made c.1760 in London.

IN THE 1770S, SUGAR NIPS WERE REPLACED BY sugar tongs, but they enjoyed a revival in the 1800s, when novelty nips – such as the Dutch doll (left) made in 1911 by Carrington & Co., London – became popular.

SIMPLE GRAPE SCISSORS WITH INSET STEEL blades appeared in the late 1700s, but most sought after are scissors dating from the Regency period and after, with the handles cast and chased in relief with trailing vines. The pair below was made of unmarked electroplate, probably in Sheffield or Birmingham, c.1850.

Length doll nips 3¾in/9.5cm   £B (doll nips); £A (others)

Sugar tongs

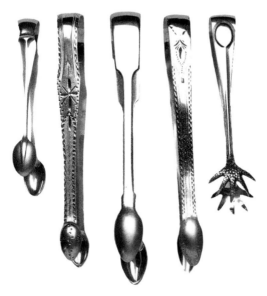

*U-SHAPED SUGAR TONGS WERE INITIALLY
constructed in three parts. The arms, often decorated
with piercing and cast and chased with gadrooning
or foliage, were soldered on to a shorter
U-shaped piece of silver engraved with a crest; most
have shell- or acorn-shaped bowls.
SUGAR TONGS MADE FROM ONE PIECE OF SILVER,
to match flatware services, were introduced in the
1780s; they were also produced in a simple
form, often enhanced with bright-cut
engraving. Unless made by a renowned maker,
sugar tongs are still inexpensive.
The tongs above were all made in London and
date, left to right, from 1905, 1785,
1800, 1792 and 1915.*

Length largest pair 5¾in/14.5cm   £A

Serving spoons

S ERVING SPOONS FIRST APPEARED IN THE
*mid-17th century, but such early specimens are now
scarce. In contemporary household inventories
or in silversmiths' accounts they were usually simply
called kitchen spoons, and the current terms –
basting spoons, gravy spoons, hash spoons and
stuffing spoons – may well be modern affectations.*

T HE EARLIEST EXAMPLES HAD TURNED WOODEN HANDLES
*or hollow "cannon" or octagonal silver handles,
but by the 1750s they were made en suite
with canteens in all patterns. Today they are usually
sold separately, falling into the category of
collector's items and, therefore, commanding much
higher prices. A rarer variety of the serving
spoon is the straining spoon, which has a pierced
divider running from the tip of the bowl to
the handle. These were used for draining vegetables
or for straining lumpy sauces.*

T HESE SERVING SPOONS WERE BOTH MADE IN LONDON,
*the example with the fruit-wood handle (top) by
Nathaniel Lock in 1715. The second piece has an
indecipherable maker's mark and dates from 1690.*
Length top spoon 15½in/39.5cm £C; £E (bottom)

Onslow pattern ladle

Ladles for serving soups, sauces and stews
were introduced in the early 1700s. The first ladles
are superb examples of the Rococo taste, their
handles terminating in cast eagle's heads or elaborate
scrolls and their bowls chased in the form of shells.
Shell fluting remained popular for some years,
although by the 1760s it was often combined with
the Hanoverian pattern and, by the 1780s, with the
Old English pattern. Throughout the 1800s, both
soup and sauce ladles were made to match the rest of
the table silver; today they are often sold separately.
This example of a shell-fluted bowl, in what is now
known as the Onslow pattern, was made
by one of the most notable Georgian silversmiths,
Hester Bateman, London, in 1772.
Length 14in/35.5cm £B

The mark of
Hester Bateman, 1761

Standing & trencher salts

Spices and condiments played an important role in the cuisine of the past. The great value placed upon salt, in particular, is reflected in the workmanship and scarce materials used to create the first salt cellars. This finely constructed, unmarked Elizabethan silver-gilt and rock-crystal standing salt on agate feet dates from c.1580.

Height 3¾in/9cm   £G

Trencher salts with shallow scooped-out containers appeared in the 1500s. Since most were made from thin sheet silver, they inevitably suffered damage and were destroyed. Some later examples, such as this unusual octagonal specimen, were made in thicker-gauge silver. It is one of a set of eight made by Noel Leonard, Paris, in 1719 and 1720.

Width 2¾in/7cm   £C; set of 8 £G

Cauldron salts

The mark of
Paul de Lamerie
*c.*1713

THE COMMONEST FORM OF SALT CELLAR IN
*the 18th century – much reproduced right up to the
present – was the cauldron salt, with a circular
moulded body raised on three or four short legs.
While most were light and delicate, particularly from
c.1750 to 1780, both earlier and later salts were
applied with cast swags of flowers and fruit, and
heavy gadrooned borders replaced dainty beaded rims
in the Regency period. The fine salt above is one of a
pair by Paul de Lamerie, London, in 1734.*
Width 3½in/9.5cm £G

THE SIMPLE SALT BELOW, BY MYER MYERS, NEW YORK,
*c.1765, is typical of those made by the thousand
in the mid-1700s. It illustrates how closely American
silver followed British silver in style at that time.*
Width 2½in/6.25cm £C; pair £E

Shell salt & pierced salt

In the early 1700s, shell salts were usually raised on tiny cast shell feet, while the Victorians mass produced thousands of small shell salts on ball feet, with matching spoons with ball terminals. Both the salts and spoon bowls were die-stamped with shell flutes and were of poor quality; nevertheless, huge numbers have survived in good condition.

The unusual shell salt above, dated 1753, is by an unknown London maker. The gilding protects the silver from the salt.

Length 4¼in/11cm £C; set of 6 £F

By the 1780s, oval salts, made from thin sheet silver, with pierced bodies and blue glass liners, were popular; British examples were often enlivened with bright-cut friezes and simple beaded or reeded rims; most are now in poor condition. This rarer specimen was probably made in Augsburg c.1785 by the German silversmith known only as Drexel.

Width 3¼in/8cm £B; pair £C

Victorian novelty salts

THE VICTORIANS LOVED *naturalism and commissioned everyday objects in bizarre novelty forms. Although despised until quite recently, these are immensely popular today, enjoying a revival as modern collectors appreciate both the quality of their construction and the sheer whimsy and fun of their design.*

THE SILVER-GILT FIGURE SALT IS FROM A *set of four by Charles F. Hancock, London, 1859, depicting four different highly romanticized "peasant" figures modelled as hunters and flower and fruit sellers. Such sets usually consist of two peasants and two noble folk, the latter more elaborately dressed than their simple counterparts.*

Height 7½in/19cm £D; set of 4 £G

ONE OF A SET OF SIX, THE DONKEY SALT *was made in 1840 by John Mortimer and John S. Hunt of London. The basket-weave panniers are gilt lined, and the bases are engraved with two crests, those of a husband and wife. This usually indicates that they were a wedding gift.*

Length 5¾in/14.5cm £D; set of 6 £G

Mustard pots I

MUSTARD WAS ORIGINALLY
*served in vase-shaped containers,
with the lids blind-pierced
or engraved with simulated
piercing to match that on
sugar casters and pepperettes.*
CONTINENTAL PIECES, SUCH AS THIS BELGIAN POT (LEFT)
*by an unknown Antwerp maker, c.1735, often had
scroll handles. This sturdy pot is chased
with arabesques, the lightness of the decoration
contrasting with the simple, elegant form.*
Height 6¾in/17cm   £E
DRUM MUSTARD POTS DATE FROM THE 18TH CENTURY.
*Some were made from sheet silver and gilt lined,
others were pierced and fitted with blue glass liners.
Both designs are still in production today. This pot
is typical of those made in the 1780s, with
bright-cut Neoclassical motifs and an elegant domed
cover. It was made in London in 1784 by the
much-collected silversmith Hester Bateman, whose
mark doubles or even triples its value.*
Height 3¾in/9.5cm   £C

Mustard pots II

*O*VAL MUSTARD POTS DECORATED WITH PIERCING
*first appeared in the 1770s. Earlier ones had vertical
sides; by the 1800s they had begun to taper, as can
be seen on this Dutch example (left) made in
Rotterdam in 1840. The piercing was done by hand –
tiny saw marks can be seen with a magnifying glass;
the edges on later die-pierced items are clean.*

Width 3in/7.5cm £B

*T*HE SPLENDID ART NOUVEAU MUSTARD POT *(RIGHT)*
*successfully combines utility with ornament.
Hand-hammered and chased with scrolls, it is studded
with cabochon amethysts and the spoon has a
matching terminal. It was designed by C.R. Ashbee
and made by the Guild of Handicraft in 1901.*

Width 2¾in/7cm £B

The mark of
the Guild of Handicraft 1900

Pepperettes

*PEPPERETTES AND SPICE
dredgers appeared in France in
the mid-17th century, reaching
Britain c.1670 and America
c.1700. The first lighthouse
peppers had plain or fluted
cylindrical bodies and steeply domed covers.
By the early 1700s, this design had been replaced by
circular or octagonal vase-shaped pieces, with tightly
fitting lids. Although this style changed little
for many decades, late 18th-century pepperettes are
flimsier than the earlier ones. The pepperette on
the left was made by James Smith, London, in 1720.*

Height 3¾in/9.5cm £C; pair £E

*THE MID-1800S SAW THE ARRIVAL OF PEPPERETTES
modelled as birds and animals or as human figures.
This curious example in the form of a knight's
helmet, the visor engraved with a crest, is by George
Unite, Birmingham, 1879. The pepper is
shaken from the eye holes to avoid spoiling the
design with holes elsewhere.*

Height 2½in/6.5cm £A; pair £B

Cruet sets

MATCHING SALTS, MUSTARDS AND PEPPERETTES
*date from the later 19th century. Although earlier
styles were much reproduced, novelty sets
were in greatest demand. This trio of chimpanzees,
made in 1867 by Edward Charles Brown,
London, is modelled in fine detail,
the apes' clothing picked out in gilding, their
eyes made from toffee-coloured glass. The mustard
pot has a matching spoon, its handle forming
the plume of the Chinese-style hat.*

Height mustard pot 4¼in/11cm   Set £E

IN THE LATE 1800S, IT WAS FASHIONABLE TO SET EACH
*place at the table with a tiny individual condiment
set. This salt pot, pepperette and butter dish were*

*made by Gorham,
Providence, Rhode
Island, in 1880.
They are engraved
in the Aesthetic
taste and enhanced
with parcel-gilding
and frosting.*

Height pepperette
3¼in/8cm   Set £C

Early cruet stand

THE EARLY 1700S SAW THE APPEARANCE OF
cruet stands fitted with an array of silver and glass
bottles and casters. Some were designed for oil
and vinegar alone, others also had salt, pepper and
mustard pots. In the 1750s, the specialist
caster maker Samuel Wood produced many cruets,
which were of the "Warwick" cinquefoil form.
Pierced circular and oval cruets, made
by a wide range of silversmiths, appeared in
the 1780s. Normally constructed from thin sheet
metal, many are now in poor condition,
with numerous splits and bruises.

THIS SPLENDID GEORGE I OIL AND VINEGAR FRAME WAS
made by Paul de Lamerie, London, in 1723. Simple
in form and yet finely pierced with pillars
and foliage, it remains totally functional 250 years
after it first graced a dining table.

Height 7¾in/19cm £G

Victorian cruet stand

CRUET STANDS BECAME LARGER AND MORE *elaborate as the 19th century progressed, with die-stamped and applied mounts, which were often hollow. The feet and handles were usually formed by die-stamping the two halves from thin silver and then soldering them together. Many cruet stands were fitted with six or eight cut-glass bottles with silver mounts or faceted ball stoppers.*

AMERICAN CRUETS WERE EVEN LARGER THAN THEIR BRITISH *counterparts – some plated examples stood as high as 18in (46cm) – and their bodies revolved around a central stem to give everyone at the table easy access to the various condiments.*

ALTHOUGH SOLID IN APPEARANCE, THIS TYPICAL VICTORIAN *cruet made in 1876 by Martin Hall and Co., Sheffield, is of poor quality, with most of the weight provided by the bottles and wooden base.*

Height 11½in/29cm £C

Charles II casters

Sugar and spice casters in sets of three
made an appearance in Britain c.1675.
As with pepperettes, the earliest examples were
of lighthouse form, their covers held on firmly
with bayonet fittings. This set has fluted
sides, which were considered more attractive as
well as being functional – the broad flutes
act like the corrugations in cardboard
to strengthen the thin metal.
The simple piercing on the covers is matched by that
on the bases, and the initials of the original owner
are crudely engraved on the side. Although
initials on later pieces of silver are unwelcome, those
on such early wares are of interest to the collector
and therefore enhance the item's value.
These casters were made by an untraced maker with
the initials W.B. in London in 1682 and 1683.
Height large caster 7in/18cm Set £G

George I casters

*T*HE OCTAGONAL FORM BECAME POPULAR
*in the early 18th century, and the shape was
adopted for items as diverse as casters, candlesticks,
coffee and teapots. The facets of plain
silver catch and reflect the light attractively, creating
subtle differences in shade, which are
often enlivened, as in these examples, by finely
engraved armorials.*

*B*Y THIS TIME, THE PIERCED DESIGNS IN THE COVERS OF
*all types of caster had become much more elaborate
and usually incorporated shells and scrolling
foliage. These were all sawn by hand – machine-
piercing with a fly-punch did not appear until
the third quarter of the 18th century.*

*T*HIS SET OF THREE GEORGE I CASTERS WAS MADE BY
Thomas Bamford in London in 1719.

Height large caster 7½in/19cm

Height smaller casters 6in/15cm   Set £F

American caster

THIS RARE AND IMPORTANT piece is the largest of only four known American sugar casters surviving from around the first quarter of the 18th century.

IT WAS MADE BY JACOBUS van der Spiegel, New York, between 1690 and 1708, probably for one John Gardiner. Van der Spiegel was of Dutch origin, and most of his wares were made in the Dutch style for Dutch émigrés, but this caster is very English in form.

Even the armorials are engraved in the British style, and it seems probable that Gardiner commissioned this unorthodox piece directly from the silversmith, rather than buying it from existing stock.

ALTHOUGH THE PIERCING IS SIMPLE, IT INCORPORATES several designs, including fleur-de-lys and hearts, and the lid is further decorated with applied cut-card work. Bayonet fittings slot into the groove at the front of the body rim, then hook over the rim, holding the lid firmly in place. The double baluster finial is more elaborate than those usually seen on British casters of this period.

Height 8¼in/21cm   £G

Vase-shaped casters

*P*LAIN VASE- AND PEAR-SHAPED CASTERS MUST
*have been made in large numbers in the 1700s, given
the plentiful supply of antique specimens seen today.
Until the 1750s, most were made from
thick-gauge silver and had elegant proportions; but
over the years the heavy cast feet were replaced by
spun domed feet, too light to provide a stable
base, so many toppled over and are covered in dents.
Heavy moulded bands were replaced by narrow
beaded or reeded bands, while the bodies began to
lose their well-balanced proportions.*
*T*HIS PAIR, MADE IN 1732 BY JOHN WHITE, LONDON,
*exemplifies the charm of the early casters; the two
together weigh almost 20 ounces (567g).*
Height 6½in/16.5cm   Pair £E

Cream jugs

First made in the reign of Queen Anne, the earliest cream jugs were similar to contemporary teapots, with octagonal bodies on domed bases. By the 1720s most were of baluster form, their cast bodies raised on shell and hoof feet, many chased with arabesques.

Quality slowly deteriorated until, by 1760, cream jugs were usually made from thin sheet silver, often bright-cut and with reed or bead borders. Many had a domed square or octagonal base, but c.1790 this style was replaced by plain oval examples with flat bases. Although these two cream jugs are similar in style, the jug below is much rarer, since the body has nine facets rather than the more usual eight.

The simplicity of the earlier jug (above), made by Gabriel Sleath c.1710, is enlivened by an engraved armorial, while the jug below, made c.1720 by David Willaume I, is chased and has a handle terminating in a serpent's head. It also has three applied feet rather than the domed base popular in the early 18th century. Both jugs bear only the maker's marks.

Height both 3½in/9cm
£D (top); £E (bottom)

Novelty cream jugs

WHOLE HERDS OF NOVELTY
jugs modelled in the Dutch
taste as cows were made by
John Schuppe, a London silversmith who probably
emigrated from the Netherlands in the
mid-18th century and who registered his mark
at Goldsmith's Hall in 1753.

THESE CREAM JUGS ARE ALMOST CARICATURES, WITH
a charming but curiously cartoonlike
appearance, unlike 19th-century cow cream jugs
which are more realistically modelled.
Schuppe made cows with plain bodies and,
more rarely, hairy bodies. Both types have tiny
hinged covers with chased foliate and
floral borders that are always enhanced
with a stylized bee.

THE TWO EXAMPLES SHOWN HERE WERE MADE IN
1761 and 1763. Although the "hairy" example
(right) has no maker's mark, it is certainly by
Schuppe; however, the absence of his punch would
depress the price considerably.

Length 5¾in/14.5cm   £F (left); £E (right)

Sauceboats

*L*ARGE BOATS FOR SAUCES AND GRAVY
*date from the early 1700s. They had cast bodies
raised on domed oval bases, a lip at each end
and two scroll handles. The more familiar
style with one lip and one handle appeared c.1730,
and domed bases were soon replaced by
shell and scroll or dolphin feet. In the main, both
19th- and 20th-century sauceboats
reproduced earlier styles.*

*T*HE PLAIN GEORGE I SAUCEBOAT (ABOVE), WITH A SIMPLE
*shaped rim, is a fairly common type. It is one of a
pair made by Joseph Sanders, London, in 1734.*

Length 8½in/21.5cm   Pair £E

*F*REDERICK KANDLER
*of London
made the ornate
sauceboat (right),
also one of a pair, in
1747. It has cast and
applied Rococo shell
and scroll borders on both
body and base, and a
shell-fluted body.*

Length 8¼in/21cm   Pair £F

Cream boat

*SMALLER BOATS FOR CREAM OR MELTED BUTTER
were produced after c.1725. Some were quite plain
but, as with sauceboats, others were cast and chased
with elaborate Rococo scrolls and shells.*

*THIS EXTRAORDINARY CREAM BOAT REPRESENTS THE ROCOCO
taste at its most extreme. The body is cast with
scales and flutes and a female figure,
and the scroll handle is finely modelled as a
serpent entwined around a branch.*

*IT IS UNMARKED, AS ARE OTHER IDENTICAL EXAMPLES THAT
can be dated to c.1735. Stylistically such pieces have
been attributed to Paul de Lamerie or Nicholas
Sprimont, both virtuoso silversmiths based in London.*

Length 4¼in/11cm   £F

The mark of
Frederick Kandler
1739 (see left)

Dutch bonbon dish

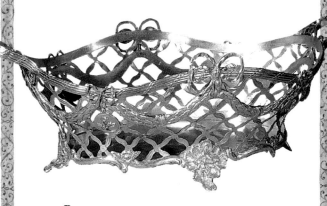

*P*IERCED BONBON DISHES WERE INTRODUCED
in the early 18th century and soon became popular.
They were used to display and serve sweetmeats,
such as crystallized fruits or ginger, and were
generally placed on the dining table during dessert.

*A*LTHOUGH BASICALLY OVAL IN SHAPE, THEIR OUTLINES
disappeared beneath a wealth of Rococo
shells and scrolls. Many were sent for assay and
hallmarking before being hand-pierced, so
it is common to find that some or all of the marks
have been partially obliterated.

*B*Y THE LATER 18TH CENTURY, BONBON DISHES WERE
of poorer quality, their thin sheet-silver bodies
pierced with fly-punches. In general, the designs are
stilted and obviously machine made, lacking
the originality of earlier dishes.

*T*HERE ARE ALWAYS EXCEPTIONS, HOWEVER, AND THIS
splendid basket, made by Johannes Jansen
of Rotterdam in 1777, is finely pierced
and engraved with trellis work and has applied
swags and reed and tie handles.

Length 6½in/16.5cm   £D

Danish bonbon dishes

THE 19TH-CENTURY SAW THE INTRODUCTION
*of mass-produced bonbon dishes, with both the
piercing and simulated chasing stamped out
by machine. These pieces were invariably lightweight
and flimsy, and most are now in poor condition,
their raised decoration often marred by tiny
holes worn in the thin metal. Most were copies of
18th-century styles, although some Art Nouveau
and Art Deco pieces can be found.*

*THESE TWO DISHES BY THE CELEBRATED DANISH SILVERSMITH
Georg Jensen, date from the early 20th century.
The tazza (right) is still in production.*

Width bowl 9¼in/23.5cm £E; Height tazza 10½in/26.5cm £E

Georg Jensen's marks
for 1914 (left) and 1915–32 (right)

Sardine dish

*A WIDE RANGE OF SPECIALIZED SERVING DISHES,
often made in electroplate largely for the wealthy and
increasingly important middle-class market, was
introduced into Britain from c.1860 to 1920.
Various items such as caviar sets with inner pots
surrounded by ice containers and asparagus dishes
complete with butter boats were produced.
Although most of these oddities are no longer used,
they are still in demand, since collectors are
amused by such relics of a bygone age.
THIS ELECTROPLATED SARDINE DISH, MADE BY WALKER AND
Hall c.1900, has a separate stand moulded with
a ledge designed to hold the serving tongs.
The "fishy" theme is maintained by the engraving
on the lid and by the "bowls" of the tongs
modelled as sardines, which were often served
as a savoury at the end of a meal.*

Length 9in/23cm £A

Butter dishes

*B*UTTER SHELLS APPEARED IN THE EARLY 1700S.
*Better-quality examples were cast and chased, with
applied periwinkle-shell feet, and some argue that
they were, in fact, used for serving shellfish.
By 1750 most were made from sheet metal, and
many have been damaged along the flutes chased
into their bowls. This shell is by John Wakelin
and William Taylor, London, 1781.*

Width 4in/10cm £B; pair £C

*C*IRCULAR COVERED BUTTER DISHES WITH COW FINIALS
*on the lids date from the early 1800s. Many were
engraved with hoops and staves to resemble
butter churns. This machine-pierced example with a
glass liner was made by Henry Wilkinson
and Co., Sheffield, 1852.*

Width 7in/18cm £C

Egg cups & cruet

IN THE 18TH AND 19TH CENTURIES EGGS WERE
*often served in cruets, or egg frames, fitted with
detachable cups and spoons, which were
both usually parcel-gilt to protect the silver from
discoloration caused by the sulphur in eggs.
Some elaborate egg cruets were even fitted with
integral salt cellars, while individual frames
that combined one or two egg cups with a small
toast rack and salt and pepper pots became popular
in the early 1800s. Single egg cups were
popular christening presents from c.1850 and
good specimens are still useful as gifts.*
THIS FINE-QUALITY GEORGE IV CRUET, WITH THE LAVISH
*mounts on the frame echoed on the cups,
was made by the London silversmith John Bridge
in 1829 and is typical of the period.*
Width 9½in/24cm £C

Toast racks

*THE EARLIEST TOAST RACKS,
dating from the mid-1700s, were
simply fashioned from
silver wire. Half a
century later, the
Regency period saw
the creation of
heavier examples,
their bases applied
with gadrooning*

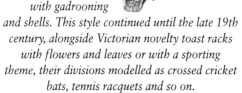

*and shells. This style continued until the late 19th
century, alongside Victorian novelty toast racks
with flowers and leaves or with a sporting
theme, their divisions modelled as crossed cricket
bats, tennis racquets and so on.*

*THE TOAST RACK ABOVE IS PART OF A LARGE VICTORIAN
breakfast set made by William Bateman and Daniel
Ball, London, in 1840. The curious electroplated
folding toast rack, influenced by the artistic
invention of the designer Christopher Dresser, was
made by Hukin and Heath, Birmingham, c.1880.*

Length Victorian toast rack 6¼in/16cm £B
Length folding toast rack 5½in/14cm £B

Napkin clip & ring

THE VICTORIANS INTRODUCED THE IDEA OF starched damask napkins as table ornaments, folding them into exotic shapes for formal dinners. The slightly soiled napkins were then ironed and used for family meals, each member's napkin marked with a silver ring that was generally initialled, although some sets were engraved with numbers.

BRITISH NAPKIN RINGS WERE SMALL, BUT HIGHLY DECORATED, mainly with engine-turning and bright-cut engraving. American rings were much more elaborate – some plated examples incorporated bud vases or condiments or had cast model children or animals applied. Indeed, the 1886–87 catalogue of The Meriden Britannia Company, Connecticut, illustrates 86 designs, from the simple to the bizarre.

THE GILT AND ENAMELLED BUTTERFLY IS A NAPKIN CLIP, part of a large set made by Tiffany and Co. in 1878 and originally used as table ornaments; the decoration varies slightly with

each. The Aesthetic movement napkin ring is by James Thompson, Sheffield, 1884.

Width clip 3¼in/8cm £B; set of 8 £G
Width napkin ring 1¼in/3cm £A

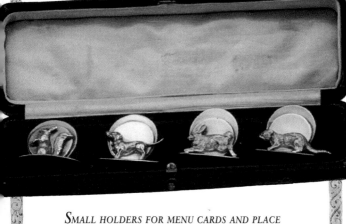

*SMALL HOLDERS FOR MENU CARDS AND PLACE
markers are still readily available. Plain discs are
least expensive, but novelty examples such as
these, featuring a squirrel, a dachshund, a hare and
an otter, are more costly. This set was made
by Sampson Mordan, London, 1911.*

Width 1¼in/3cm Set £B

*SILVER KNIFE RESTS, DESIGNED TO PREVENT GREASE
marking the table, appeared in the late 1700s; they
were made from wire and were triangular in
section. By the early 1800s, the bar with
two X-shaped supports had evolved; most had
simple legs but some were more lavish.
From c.1850 examples with bars supported by
animals appeared. This pair,
by Walker and Hall,
Sheffield, was made in
1904, but the design
harks back to the early 1800s.*

Width 3in/7.5cm £A

Early wine goblets

SIXTEENTH-CENTURY WINE GOBLETS ARE
*extremely rare. They were made from thin beaten
sheet silver, which made them prone to damage –
their bowls and domed bases split quite easily, even
with careful use. Most were simple in form, with
plain tapering bowls sometimes enlivened by
engraved friezes of stylized foliage and naive flower
heads, animals, birds and insects.*

THE LARGE ELIZABETHAN CUP ON THE RIGHT IS DECORATED
*in this manner, with a narrow engraved frieze.
It was made at Norwich in 1567 by an
unidentified maker.*

Height 5¾in/14.5cm   £E

GILBERT SHEPHERD OF LONDON PROBABLY PRODUCED THE
*smaller Commonwealth cup (left) which dates
from 1655. This has a broad chased frieze of tulips
within arched scroll panels, and the design is
finished off with a punched bead border.*

Height 3¼in/8cm   £E

Later goblets

By the mid- to late 18th century, goblets
were produced in large sets, although most have been
broken up and antique goblets are now usually
sold singly. Odd goblets from a specific period can,
however, be matched quite successfully, since
they vary only slightly in shape, size and decoration.
From c.1760 to 1790 most stood on circular bases,
and beaded borders and bright-cut swags of
bows, flowers and foliage were popular. This goblet
was made by Thomas Daniel, London, in 1784.

Height 7in/18cm £B

At the turn of the century, silversmiths competing
with the makers of Old Sheffield plate introduced
square bases, since they realized the plate makers
would have difficulty hiding the red base-metal
edges where two pieces of plated copper were joined.
But by 1810 the plate makers had solved this
problem, so circular bases reappeared, combined
with campana-shaped bowls.

Wine & spirit labels

LABELS FOR WINES AND SPIRITS, SOME PLAIN,
others chased with vines, appeared in the 1730s. By
the 1750s there were two main types: gadrooned
oblong examples and cast labels with Rococo
decoration. In the Regency period labels were highly
ornate, to show up against the deeply cut glass
decanters then fashionable. Silver labels began
to disappear in 1860, when it became legal to sell
alcohol in bottles with paper labels.

SOME COLLECTORS LOOK FOR LABELS WITH UNUSUAL SHAPES,
with titles such as Hollands and Nig (euphemisms
for gin), or with bizarre spellings, such as Clairret;
but, in general, sets are more valuable than
individual examples. Peter and William Bateman,
London, made the Hollands label, one of a set of six,
in 1806. The silver-gilt Madeira label is one of a set
of eight by Philip Rundell, London, 1819.

Width Hollands label 2in/5cm; Madeira label 2¾in/7cm   £A

Wine coasters

FROM THE 1760s, WINE coasters were produced in large numbers. The earliest had bright-cut or pierced silver gallery sides and mahogany bases with green baize underneath to prevent the table being scratched.

INITIALLY THEY WERE QUITE SMALL, BUT THEIR SIZE increased to hold larger decanters, and their silver mounts became increasingly elaborate, until, by the Regency period, they were often made of silver-gilt with die-stamped vine friezes and acanthus leaf or gadroon borders. The wooden bases were also often inset with bosses to accommodate the engraved crests of their owners. Single silver coasters are still quite inexpensive, since most collectors prefer pairs or larger sets.

THE SPLENDID SILVER COASTER ABOVE, WITH VINE leaves cut out and soldered into place individually, is one of four by Joseph Cradock and William Ker Reid, London, 1818.

Width 6½in/16.5cm

£B; pair £E

VICTORIAN COASTERS were usually simpler; this elegant electroplate one (right) was made by Elkington and Co., Birmingham, in 1860.

Width 7in/18cm £A; pair £B

Table bells 1

*ALTHOUGH SERVANTS WERE PRESENT DURING
formal dinners, more intimate occasions demanded
privacy so that the diners could flirt or exchange
gossip. Family meals were also much less formal, and
people often helped themselves from dishes on the
sideboard. The servants would be called in to bring
the next course by ringing a table bell.*

*THE EARLIEST, DATING FROM THE REIGN OF GEORGE II,
had baluster handles and cast bodies. This design
was made throughout the 18th and 19th
centuries, but later specimens often have ivory
handles. Many novelty bells were also made in the
19th century, some with inexpensive
die-stamped handles and mounts applied to
glass or base-metal bodies.*

The 1897 mark of
G.R. Elkington & Co.,
who patented the
electroplating process
in 1840.

Table bells II

THE BELL WITH LEAF AND TENDRIL HANDLE
*(far left) was made from very thin silver by Van
Kempen en Zn., Voorschoten, Netherlands, in 1882.
It is badly made, with a flimsy handle,
but its tone is attractive, since the "tinny" body
covers a more solid plated bell.*

MADE C.1880 BY ELKINGTON & CO. OF BIRMINGHAM, THE
*electroplate bell (left) is cast in the form of an old lady
with poke bonnet, shawls and a lap dog.*

A CLOSE COPY OF AN 18TH-CENTURY BELL, THE EXAMPLE
*below has a turned ivory baluster handle, a body
cast and chased with foliage and a
moulded band. It was made in 1928
by Crichton Brothers, London, who
specialized in reproduction pieces.*

Height all bells 6–6½in/15–16.5cm £B

THE TORTOISE (ABOVE) HAS A CAST METAL
*body and a silver head, tail and
die-stamped shell. It is fitted with a
spring wound up with a concealed
key and, when the head or tail is
pressed, produces a buzzing
ring. It was made by Nathan
and Hayes, Chester, in 1908.*

Length 6½in/16.5cm £B

Glossary

ASSAY To test a silver alloy to ensure it comes up to standard.

BEADING An ornamental edging, made up of tiny half-spheres, or beads, which was popular in the late 18th century.

BRIGHT-CUT ENGRAVING A type of engraving using a double-edged tool to remove slivers of metal and burnish the cut at the same time.

CHASING Technique of decorating silver using a hammer or blunt punch to raise or depress the surface, leaving a design in relief.

ELECTROPLATING An electro-chemical method of plating metal, usually copper, in which a thin layer of silver is deposited, forming a tightly bonded skin on the base. It was developed by George and Frederick Elkington in the mid-1800s.

EMBOSSING Decoration formed by raising a design from behind using a blunt punch. The result is similar to chasing.

ENGRAVING Decoration in which lines or dots are incised into the surface by means of a diamond-tipped tool, a spinning abrasive wheel or acid.

FEATHER EDGE Engraving that looks like the barbs of a feather; often used on the handles of cutlery.

FINIAL A decorative knob on the top of an object.

FLATWARE A general term for cutlery formed from flat metal sheets.

FROSTING A finely textured decorative finish used to contrast with polished silver.

GILDING The coating of silver with a thin film of gold for decoration or to protect it from the harmful effects of egg, salt or fruit juices.

MONOGRAM Overlapping initials that create a decorative design.

OLD SHEFFIELD PLATE, also known as fused plate. In 1743, Thomas Boulsover discovered that if a thin layer of silver was fused to copper then rolled into a flat sheet, the two metals could be worked as one to provide a cheap alternative to silver. After an object was made, silver wire was soldered over the exposed edges to conceal the copper. (*See p.75*)

PARCEL-GILT Silver that is partly gilded.

QUATREFOIL A shape with four sides; similar to a four-leafed clover.

RAT-TAIL A short ridge of silver applied to the back of spoon bowls to reinforce the joint with the handle.

REEDING Narrow grooved strips generally used as a decorative border.

REPOUSSÉ Term used to describe a raised design created with a hammer and punch, which is then "pushed back" in places to give modelling to the design.

Index

Acknowledgments

All pictures courtesy of Christie's South Kensington except for the following:
Christie's Images: 6–7; 11–17; 21–23; 26–27; 44; 46–47t; 48t; 49–50l; 52l; 54; 56–57; 59–65; 68–69t; 72; 74r–75t.
Christie's New York: 24–25; 33; 34; 35–38l; 47r; 53b; 58.
Clive Corless/Marshall Editions: 32b; 40; 43; 45; 51; 55; 66–67t; 69b.
Mansell Collection: 9. National Trust Photographic Library/ Andreas von Einsiedel: 8.
Illustrators: **Carol Hill** (borders & marks), **Debbie Hinks** (endpapers).